United States Government Accountability Office

Testimony

Before the Committee on Homeland Security and Governmental Affairs, U.S. Senate

For Release on Delivery
Expected at 10:00 a.m. EDT
Thursday, October 31, 2013

PERSONNEL SECURITY CLEARANCES

Full Development and Implementation of Metrics Needed to Measure Quality of Process

Statement of Brenda S. Farrell, Director
Defense Capabilities and Management

I0448689

GAO-14-157T

GAO
Highlights

Highlights of GAO-14-157T, a testimony before the Committee on Homeland Security and Governmental Affairs, U.S. Senate

PERSONNEL SECURITY CLEARANCES

Full Development and Implementation of Metrics Needed to Measure Quality of Process

Why GAO Did This Study

A high-quality personnel security clearance process is necessary to minimize the associated risks of unauthorized disclosures of classified information and to help ensure that information about individuals with criminal activity or other questionable behavior is identified and assessed as part of the process for granting or retaining clearances. Personnel security clearances allow individuals access to classified information that, through unauthorized disclosure, can in some cases cause exceptionally grave damage to U.S. national security. In 2012, the DNI reported that more than 4.9 million federal government and contractor employees held or were eligible to hold a security clearance. GAO has reported that the federal government spent over $1 billion to conduct background investigations (in support of security clearances and suitability determinations—the consideration of character and conduct for federal employment) in fiscal year 2011.

This testimony addresses the (1) overall security clearance process, including roles and responsibilities; and (2) extent that executive branch agencies have metrics to help determine the quality of the security clearance process. This testimony is based on GAO work issued between 2008 and 2013 on DOD's personnel security clearance program and governmentwide suitability and security clearance reform efforts. As part of that work, GAO (1) reviewed statutes, federal guidance, and processes, (2) examined agency data on the timeliness and quality of investigations and adjudications, (3) assessed reform efforts, and (4) reviewed samples of case files for DOD personnel.

View GAO-14-157T. For more information, contact Brenda S. Farrell at (202) 512-3604 or FarrellB@gao.gov.

What GAO Found

Multiple executive branch agencies are responsible for different steps of the multi-phased personnel security clearance process that includes: determination of whether a position requires a clearance, application submission, investigation, and adjudication. Agency officials must first determine whether a federal civilian position requires access to classified information. The Director of National Intelligence (DNI) and the Office of Personnel Management (OPM) are in the process of issuing a joint revision to the regulations guiding this step in response to GAO's 2012 recommendation that the DNI issue policy and guidance for the determination, review, and validation of requirements. After an individual has been selected for a federal civilian position that requires a personnel security clearance and the individual submits an application for a clearance, investigators—often contractors—from OPM conduct background investigations for most executive branch agencies. Adjudicators from requesting agencies use the information from these investigations and consider federal adjudicative guidelines to determine whether an applicant is eligible for a clearance. Further, individuals are subject to reinvestigations at intervals that are dependent on the level of security clearance. For example, top secret and secret clearance holders are to be reinvestigated every 5 years and 10 years, respectively.

Executive branch agencies have not fully developed and implemented metrics to measure quality throughout the personnel security clearance process. For more than a decade, GAO has emphasized the need to build and monitor quality throughout the personnel security clearance process to promote oversight and positive outcomes such as maximizing the likelihood that individuals who are security risks will be scrutinized more closely. For example, GAO reported in May 2009 that, with respect to initial top secret clearances adjudicated in July 2008 for the Department of Defense (DOD), documentation was incomplete for most of OPM's investigative reports. GAO independently estimated that 87 percent of about 3,500 investigative reports that DOD adjudicators used to make clearance eligibility decisions were missing some required documentation, such as the verification of all of the applicant's employment. GAO also estimated that 12 percent of the 3,500 reports did not contain the required personal subject interview. In 2009, GAO recommended that OPM measure the frequency with which its investigative reports met federal investigative standards in order to improve the quality of investigation documentation. As of August 2013, however, OPM had not implemented this recommendation. GAO's 2009 report also identified issues with the quality of DOD adjudications. Specifically, GAO estimated that 22 percent of about 3,500 initial top secret clearances that were adjudicated favorably did not contain all the required documentation. As a result, in 2009 GAO recommended that DOD measure the frequency with which adjudicative files meet requirements. In November 2009, DOD issued a memorandum that established a tool called the Review of Adjudication Documentation Accuracy and Rationales (RADAR) to measure the frequency with which adjudicative files meet the requirements of DOD regulation. According to a DOD official, RADAR had been used in fiscal year 2010 to evaluate some adjudications, but was not used in fiscal year 2011 due to funding shortfalls. DOD restarted the use of RADAR in fiscal year 2012.

_____ **United States Government Accountability Office**

Chairman Carper, Ranking Member Coburn, and Members of the Committee:

Thank you for the opportunity to be here to participate in this discussion of the federal government's process for personnel security clearances. A high-quality personnel security clearance process is necessary to minimize the associated risks of unauthorized disclosures of classified information and to help ensure that information about individuals with criminal activity or other questionable behavior is identified and assessed as part of the process for granting or retaining clearances. However, recent events, such as unauthorized disclosures of classified information, have shown that there is more work to be done by federal agencies to help ensure the process functions effectively and efficiently, so that only trustworthy individuals obtain and keep security clearances and the resulting access to classified information that clearances make possible.

As you know, we have an extensive body of work on issues related to the personnel security clearance process going back over a decade. Since 2008, we have focused on the government-wide effort to reform the security clearance process. Personnel security clearances allow government and industry personnel (contractors) to gain access to classified information that, through unauthorized disclosure, can in some cases cause exceptionally grave damage to U.S. national security. It is important to keep in mind that security clearances allow for access to classified information on a need to know basis. Federal agencies also use other processes and procedures to determine if an individual should be granted access to certain government buildings or facilities or be employed as either a military, federal civilian employee, or contractor for the federal government. Separate from, but related to, personnel security clearances are determinations of suitability that the executive branch uses to ensure individuals are suitable, based on character and conduct, for federal employment in their agency or position.

The federal government processes a high volume of personnel security clearances at significant costs. In 2012, the Director of National Intelligence (DNI) reported that more than 4.9 million federal government and contractor employees held or were eligible to hold a security clearance, which poses a formidable challenge to those responsible for deciding who should be granted a clearance. Furthermore, the federal government spent over $1 billion to conduct more than 2 million background investigations (in support of both personnel security clearances and suitability determinations for government employment outside of the intelligence community) in fiscal year 2011. The

Department of Defense (DOD) accounts for the majority of all personnel security clearances—which includes 788,000 background investigations that cost over $787 million in fiscal year 2011.[1]

My testimony today will focus on two topics related to personnel security clearances. First, I will discuss the overall personnel security clearance process, including roles and responsibilities for investigations and adjudications. Second, I will discuss the extent that executive branch agencies have developed and implemented metrics to help determine the quality of the security clearance process.

My testimony is based on our reports and testimonies issued from 2008 through 2013 on DOD's personnel security clearance program and government-wide suitability and security clearance reform efforts. A list of these related products appears at the end of my statement. As part of the work for these products, we reviewed statutes, federal guidance and processes, examined agency data on the timeliness and quality of investigations and adjudications, assessed reform efforts, and reviewed a sample of investigative and adjudication files for DOD personnel. The work upon which this testimony is based was conducted in accordance with generally accepted government auditing standards. Those standards require that we plan and perform the audit to obtain sufficient, appropriate evidence to provide a reasonable basis for our findings and conclusions based on our audit objectives. We believe that the evidence obtained provides a reasonable basis for our findings and conclusions based on our audit objectives. Further details about the scope and methodology can be found in each of these related products.

The Overall Personnel Security Clearance Process

Multiple executive-branch agencies have key roles and responsibilities for different steps of the federal government's personnel security clearance process. For example, in 2008, Executive Order 13467[2] designated the DNI as the Security Executive Agent. As such, the DNI is responsible for developing policies and procedures to help ensure the effective, efficient,

---

[1]GAO, *Background Investigations: Office of Personnel Management Needs to Improve Transparency of Its Pricing and Seek Cost Savings*, GAO-12-197 (Washington, D.C.: Feb. 28, 2012).

[2]Executive Order No. 13467, *Reforming Processes Related to Suitability for Government Employment, Fitness for Contractor Employees, and Eligibility for Access to Classified National Security Information* (June 30, 2008).

and timely completion of background investigations and adjudications relating to determinations of eligibility for access to classified information and eligibility to hold a sensitive position. In turn, executive branch agencies determine which of their positions—military, civilian, or private-industry contractors—require access to classified information and, therefore, which people must apply for and undergo a personnel security clearance investigation. Investigators—often contractors—from Federal Investigative Services within the Office of Personnel Management (OPM)[3] conduct these investigations for most of the federal government using federal investigative standards and OPM internal guidance as criteria for collecting background information on applicants.[4] OPM provides the resulting investigative reports to the requesting agencies for their internal adjudicators, who use the information along with the federal adjudicative guidelines to determine whether an applicant is eligible for a personnel security clearance. DOD is OPM's largest customer, and its Under Secretary of Defense for Intelligence (USD(I)) is responsible for developing, coordinating, and overseeing the implementation of DOD policy, programs, and guidance for personnel, physical, industrial, information, operations, chemical/biological, and DOD Special Access Program security. Additionally, the Defense Security Service, under the authority, direction, and control of USD(I), manages and administers the

---

[3] OPM's Federal Investigative Services employs both federal and contract investigators to conduct work required to complete background investigations. The federal staff constitutes about 25 percent of that workforce, while OPM currently also has contracts for investigative fieldwork with several investigation firms, constituting the remaining 75 percent of its investigative workforce.

[4] In 2005, the Office of Management and Budget designated OPM as the agency responsible for, among other things, the day-to-day supervision and monitoring of security clearance investigations, and for tracking the results of individual agency-performed adjudications, subject to certain exceptions. However, the Office of the Director of National Intelligence can designate other agencies as an "authorized investigative agency" pursuant to 50 U.S.C. § 3341(b)(3), as implemented through Executive Order 13467. Alternatively, under 5 U.S.C. § 1104(a)(2), OPM can redelegate any of its investigative functions subject to performance standards and a system of oversight prescribed by OPM under 5 U.S.C. § 1104(b). Agencies without delegated authority rely on OPM to conduct their background investigations while agencies with delegated authority—including the Defense Intelligence Agency, National Security Agency, National Geospatial-Intelligence Agency, Central Intelligence Agency, Federal Bureau of Investigation, National Reconnaissance Office, and Department of State—have been authorized to conduct their own background investigations.

DOD portion of the National Industrial Security Program[5] for the DOD components and other federal agencies by agreement, as well as providing security education and training, among other things.

Section 3001 of the Intelligence Reform and Terrorism Prevention Act of 2004[6] prompted government-wide suitability and security clearance reform. The act required, among other matters, an annual report to Congress—in February of each year from 2006 through 2011—about progress and key measurements on the timeliness of granting security clearances. It specifically required those reports to include the periods of time required for conducting investigations and adjudicating or granting clearances. However, the Intelligence Reform and Terrorism Prevention Act requirement for the executive branch to annually report on its timeliness expired in 2011. More recently the Intelligence Authorization Act of 2010[7] established a new requirement that the President annually report to Congress the total amount of time required to process certain security clearance determinations for the previous fiscal year for each element of the Intelligence Community.[8] The Intelligence Authorization Act of 2010 additionally requires that those annual reports include the total number of active security clearances throughout the United States government, to include both government employees and contractors. Unlike the Intelligence Reform and Terrorism Prevention Act of 2004 reporting requirement, the requirement to submit these annual reports does not expire.

In 2007, DOD and the Office of the Director of National Intelligence (ODNI) formed the Joint Security Clearance Process Reform Team, known as the Joint Reform Team, to improve the security clearance process government-wide. In a 2008 memorandum, the President called for a reform of the security clearance and suitability determination

---

[5]The National Industrial Security Program was established by Executive Order 12829 to safeguard Federal Government classified information that is released to contractors, licensees, and grantees of the United States Government. Executive Order 12829, *National Industrial Security Program* (Jan. 6, 1993, as amended).

[6]Pub. L. No. 108-458 (2004) (relevant sections codified at 50 U.S.C. § 3341).

[7]Pub. L. No. 111-259, § 367 (2010) (codified at 50 U.S.C. § 3104).

[8]This timeliness reporting requirement applies only to the elements of the Intelligence Community; it does not cover non-intelligence agencies that were covered by the reporting requirements in the Intelligence Reform and Terrorism Prevention Act of 2004.

processes and subsequently issued Executive Order 13467,[9] which in addition to designating the DNI as the Security Executive Agent, also designated the Director of OPM as the Suitability Executive Agent. Specifically, the Director of OPM, as Suitability Executive Agent, is responsible for developing policies and procedures to help ensure the effective, efficient, and timely completion of investigations and adjudications relating to determinations of suitability, to include consideration of an individual's character or conduct. Further, the executive order established a Suitability and Security Clearance Performance Accountability Council to oversee agency progress in implementing the reform vision. Under the executive order, this council is accountable to the President for driving implementation of the reform effort, including ensuring the alignment of security and suitability processes, holding agencies accountable for implementation, and establishing goals and metrics for progress. The order also appointed the Deputy Director for Management at the Office of Management and Budget as the chair of the council.[10]

Steps in the Personnel Security Clearance Process

In the first step of the personnel security clearance process, executive branch officials determine the requirements of a federal civilian position, including assessing the risk and sensitivity level associated with that position, to determine whether it requires access to classified information and, if required, the level of access. Security clearances are generally categorized into three levels: top secret, secret, and confidential.[11] The level of classification denotes the degree of protection required for information and the amount of damage that unauthorized disclosure could

---

[9]Executive Order No. 13467, *Reforming Processes Related to Suitability for Government Employment, Fitness for Contractor Employees, and Eligibility for Access to Classified National Security Information* (June 30, 2008).

[10]The Performance Accountability Council is comprised of the Director of National Intelligence as the Security Executive Agent, the Director of OPM as the Suitability Executive Agent, and the Deputy Director for Management, Office of Management and Budget, as the chair with the authority to designate officials from additional agencies to serve as members. As of June 2012, the council included representatives from the Departments of Defense, Energy, Health and Human Services, Homeland Security, State, Treasury, and Veterans Affairs, and the Federal Bureau of Investigation.

[11]A top secret clearance is generally also required for access to Sensitive Compartmented Information—classified intelligence information concerning or derived from intelligence sources, methods, or analytical processes that is required to be protected within formal access control systems established and overseen by the Director of National Intelligence.

reasonably be expected to cause to national defense or foreign relations. A sound requirements process is important because requests for clearances for positions that do not need a clearance or need a lower level of clearance increase investigative workloads and costs. In 2012, we reported that the DNI, as the Security Executive Agent, had not provided agencies clearly defined policy and procedures to consistently determine if a position requires a security clearance, or established guidance to require agencies to review and revise or validate existing federal civilian position designations.[12] We recommended that the DNI issue policy and guidance for the determination, review, and validation of requirements, and ODNI concurred with those recommendations, stating that it recognized the need to issue or clarify policy. Currently, OPM and ODNI are in the process of issuing a joint revision to the regulations guiding requirements determination. Specifically, according to officials from the ODNI, these offices had obtained permission from the President to re-issue the federal regulation jointly, drafted the proposed rule, and obtained public input on the regulation by publishing it in the Federal Register. According to ODNI and OPM officials, they will jointly review and address comments and prepare the final rule for approval from the Office of Management and Budget.

Once an applicant is selected for a position that requires a personnel security clearance, the applicant must obtain a security clearance in order to gain access to classified information. While different departments and agencies may have slightly different personnel security clearance processes, the phases that follow—application submission, investigation, and adjudication—are illustrative of a typical process.[13] Since 1997, federal agencies have followed a common set of personnel security investigative standards and adjudicative guidelines for determining whether federal civilian workers, military personnel, and others, such as private industry personnel contracted by the government, are eligible to hold a security clearance. Figure 1 illustrates the steps in the personnel security clearance process, which is representative of the general

---

[12]GAO, *Security Clearances: Agencies Need Clearly Defined Policy for Determining Civilian Position Requirements,* GAO-12-800 (Washington, D.C.: July 12, 2012).

[13]The general process for performing a background investigation for either a secret or top secret clearance is the same; however, the level of detail and types of information gathered for a top secret clearance is more substantial than a secret clearance.

process followed by most executive branch agencies and includes procedures for appeals and renewals.

Figure 1: Steps in the Personnel Security Clearance Process

Requirements determination.
Executive branch agencies determine a position's level of sensitivity, which includes consideration of whether or not a position requires access to classified information and, if required, the level of access. This information helps inform the decision as to whether a clearance is needed. Employees in these positions must be able to obtain and maintain a security clearance to gain access to classified information.

Application.
If, during the requirements determination phase, an agency determines that a position requires a clearance, the employee completes an electronic standard form 86 application, which the requesting agency sends to the Office of Personnel Management (OPM).

Investigation.
OPM's Federal Investigative Services division—with a workforce that is 25 percent federal investigator staff and 75 percent contract investigator staff—use federal investigative standards and OPM's internal guidance to conduct the investigations.

Adjudication.
Adjudicators from the requesting agency use the information from the investigative report to determine whether to grant or deny the employee eligibility for a security clearance by considering guidelines in 13 specific areas that elicit information about (1) conduct that could raise security concerns and (2) factors that could allay those security concerns and permit granting a clearance.

Appeals.
If an adjudicator determines that the agency should deny an initial security clearance application or revoke an existing security clearance, an employee may appeal. The appeals process varies depending on a variety of factors, and may involve agency adjudicators, security appeals boards, and, in some cases, the Defense Office of Hearings and Appeals.

Periodic reinvestigation.
As long as an individual holding a personnel security clearance remains in a position requiring access to classified information, that individual is reinvestigated periodically at intervals dependent on the level of security clearance. Top secret clearance holders are reinvestigated every 5 years and secret clearance holders are reinvestigated every 10 years.

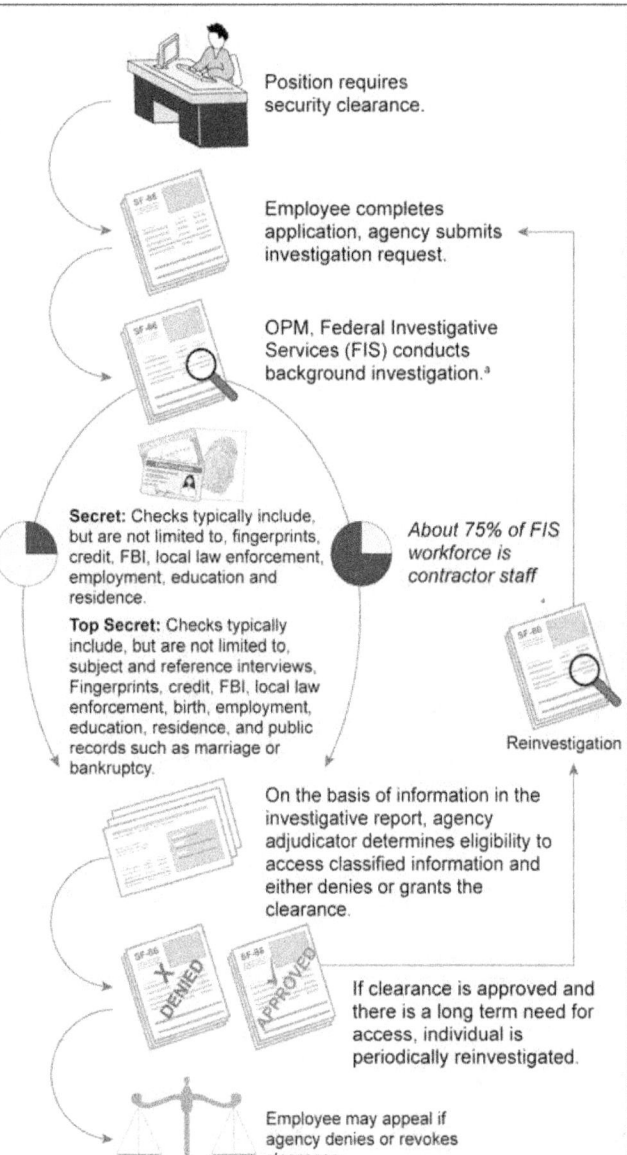

Position requires security clearance.

Employee completes application, agency submits investigation request.

OPM, Federal Investigative Services (FIS) conducts background investigation.[a]

About 25% of FIS workforce is federal staff

Secret: Checks typically include, but are not limited to, fingerprints, credit, FBI, local law enforcement, employment, education and residence.

Top Secret: Checks typically include, but are not limited to, subject and reference interviews, Fingerprints, credit, FBI, local law enforcement, birth, employment, education, residence, and public records such as marriage or bankruptcy.

About 75% of FIS workforce is contractor staff

Reinvestigation

On the basis of information in the investigative report, agency adjudicator determines eligibility to access classified information and either denies or grants the clearance.

If clearance is approved and there is a long term need for access, individual is periodically reinvestigated.

Employee may appeal if agency denies or revokes clearance.

Source: GAO analysis.

[a]OPM provides background investigation services to over 100 executive branch agencies; however, others, including some agencies in the Intelligence Community, have been delegated authority from the Office of the Director of National Intelligence, OPM, or both, to conduct their own background investigations.

During the application submission phase, a security officer from an executive branch agency (1) requests an investigation of an individual requiring a clearance; (2) forwards a personnel security questionnaire (Standard Form 86) using OPM's electronic Questionnaires for Investigations Processing (e-QIP) system or a paper copy of the Standard Form 86 to the individual to complete; (3) reviews the completed questionnaire; and (4) sends the questionnaire and supporting documentation, such as fingerprints and signed waivers, to OPM or its investigation service provider.

During the investigation phase, investigators—often contractors—from OPM's Federal Investigative Services use federal investigative standards and OPM's internal guidance to conduct and document the investigation of the applicant. The scope of information gathered in an investigation depends on the needs of the client agency and the personnel security clearance requirements of an applicant's position, as well as whether the investigation is for an initial clearance or a reinvestigation to renew a clearance. For example, in an investigation for a top secret clearance, investigators gather additional information through more time-consuming efforts, such as traveling to conduct in-person interviews to corroborate information about an applicant's employment and education. However, many background investigation types have similar components. For instance, for all investigations, information that applicants provide on electronic applications are checked against numerous databases. Both secret and top secret investigations contain credit and criminal history checks, while top secret investigations also contain citizenship, public record, and spouse checks as well as reference interviews and an Enhanced Subject Interview to gain insight into an applicant's character. Table 1 highlights the investigative components generally associated with the secret and top secret clearance levels. After OPM, or the designated provider, completes the background investigation, the resulting investigative report is provided to the adjudicating agency.

Table 1: Information Gathered in Conducting a Typical Investigation to Determine Suitability and Eligibility for a Personnel Security Clearance

Type of information gathered by component	Type of background investigation	
	Secret	Top Secret
1. Personnel security questionnaire: The reported answers on an electronic SF-85P or SF-86 form	X	X
2. Fingerprints: Fingerprints submitted electronically or manually	X	X
3. National agency check: Data from Federal Bureau of Investigation, military records, and other agencies as required (with fingerprint)	X	X
4. Credit check: Data from credit bureaus where the subject lived/worked/attended school for at least 6 months	X	X
5. Local agency checks: Data from law enforcement agencies where the subject lived/worked/attended school during the past 10 years or—in the case of reinvestigations—since the last security clearance investigation	X	X
6. Date and place of birth: Corroboration of information supplied on the personnel security questionnaire		X
7. Citizenship: For individuals born outside of the United States, verification of U.S. citizenship directly from the appropriate registration authority		X
8. Education: Verification of most recent or significant claimed attendance, degree, or diploma	V	X
9. Employment: Review of employment records and interviews with workplace references, such as supervisors and coworkers	V	X
10. References: Data from interviews with subject-identified and investigator-developed leads	V	X
11. National agency check for spouse or cohabitant: Data from Federal Bureau of Investigation, military records, and other agencies as required (without fingerprint)		X
12. Former spouse: Data from interview(s) conducted with spouse(s) divorced within the last 10 years or since the last investigation or reinvestigation		X
13. Neighborhoods: Interviews with neighbors and verification of residence through records check	V	X
14. Public records: Verification of issues, such as bankruptcy, divorce, and criminal and civil court cases		X
15. Enhanced Subject Interview: Collection of relevant data, resolution of significant issues or inconsistencies	a	X

Source: DOD and OPM

Note: The content and amount of information collected as part of a personnel security clearance investigation is dependent on a variety of case-specific factors, including the history of the applicant and the nature of the position; however, items 1-15 are typically collected for the types of investigations indicated.

V = Components with this notation are checked through a mail voucher sent by OPM's Federal Investigative Services.

[a]The Enhanced Subject Interview was developed by the Joint Reform Team and implemented by OPM in 2011 and serves as an in-depth discussion between the interviewer and the subject to ensure a full understanding of the applicant's information, potential issues, and mitigating factors. It is included in a Minimum Background Investigation, one type of suitability investigation, and can be triggered by the presence of issues in a secret level investigation.

During the adjudication phase, adjudicators from the hiring agency[14] use the information from the investigative report to determine whether an applicant is eligible for a security clearance. To make clearance eligibility decisions, the adjudication guidelines specify that adjudicators consider 13 specific areas that elicit information about (1) conduct that could raise security concerns and (2) factors that could allay those security concerns and permit granting a clearance.[15] If a clearance is denied or revoked, appeals of the adjudication decision are possible. We have work underway to review the process for security revocations. We expect to issue a report on this process by spring of 2014.

Once an individual has obtained a personnel security clearance and as long as they remain in a position that requires access to classified national security information, that individual is reinvestigated periodically at intervals that are dependent on the level of security clearance. For example, top secret clearance holders are reinvestigated every 5 years, and secret clearance holders are reinvestigated every 10 years. Some of the information gathered during a reinvestigation would focus specifically

---

[14]For industry personnel, the Defense Security Service (DSS) adjudicated clearance eligibility for DOD and 24 other federal agencies, by agreement, using OPM-provided investigative reports. However, DOD is in the process of consolidating its adjudication facilities, including those for industry personnel. Per DOD 5220.22-M, *National Industrial Security Program: Operating Manual* (Feb. 28, 2006 incorporating changes Mar. 28, 2013), those agencies are: (1) National Aeronautics and Space Administration; (2) Department of Commerce; (3) General Services Administration; (4) Department of State; (5) Small Business Administration; (6) National Science Foundation; (7) Department of the Treasury; (8) Department of Transportation; (9) Department of the Interior; (10) Department of Agriculture; (11) Department of Labor; (12) Environmental Protection Agency; (13) Department of Justice; (14) Federal Reserve System; (15) Government Accountability Office; (16) U.S. Trade Representative; (17) U.S. International Trade Commission; (18) U.S. Agency for International Development; (19) Nuclear Regulatory Commission; (20) Department of Education; (21) Department of Health and Human Services; (22) Department of Homeland Security; (23) Federal Communications Commission; and (24) Office of Personnel Management.

[15]Federal guidelines state that clearance decisions require a common sense determination of eligibility for access to classified information based upon careful consideration of the following 13 areas: allegiance to the United States; foreign influence; foreign preference; sexual behavior; personal conduct; financial considerations; alcohol consumption; drug involvement; emotional, mental, and personality disorders; criminal conduct; security violations; outside activities; and misuse of information technology systems. Further, the guidelines require adjudicators to evaluate the relevance of an individual's overall conduct by considering factors such as the nature, extent, and seriousness of the conduct; the circumstances surrounding the conduct, to include knowledgeable participation; the frequency and recency of the conduct; and the individual's age and maturity at the time of the conduct, among others.

on the period of time since the last approved clearance, such as a check of local law enforcement agencies where an individual lived and worked since the last investigation. Further, the Joint Reform Team began an effort to review the possibility of continuous evaluations, which would ascertain on a more frequent basis whether an eligible employee with access to classified information continues to meet the requirements for access. Specifically, the team proposed to move from periodic review to that of continuous evaluation, meaning annually for top secret and similar positions and at least once every five years for secret or similar positions, as a means to reveal security-relevant information earlier than the previous method, and provide increased scrutiny on populations that could potentially represent risk to the government because they already have access to classified information. The current federal investigative standards state that the top secret level of security clearances may be subject to continuous evaluation.

Full Development and Implementation of Metrics Needed to Determine Quality of Personnel Security Clearance Process

The executive branch has developed some metrics to assess quality at different phases of the personnel security clearance process; however, those metrics have not been fully developed and implemented. To promote oversight and positive outcomes, such as maximizing the likelihood that individuals who are security risks will be scrutinized more closely, we have emphasized, since the late 1990s,[16] the need to build and monitor quality throughout the personnel security clearance process. Having assessment tools and performance metrics in place is a critical initial step toward instituting a program to monitor and independently validate the effectiveness and sustainability of corrective measures. However, we have previously reported that executive branch agencies have not fully developed and implemented metrics to measure quality in key aspects of the personnel security clearance process, including: (1) investigative reports; (2) adjudicative files; and (3) the reciprocity of personnel security clearances, which is an agency's acceptance of a background investigation or clearance determination completed by any authorized investigative or adjudicative executive branch agency.

---

[16]GAO, *DOD Personnel: Inadequate Personnel Security Investigations Pose National Security Risks,* GAO/NSIAD-00-12 (Washington, D.C.: Oct. 27, 1999).

Metrics Not Yet Implemented to Measure Completeness of OPM Investigative Reports

We have previously identified deficiencies in OPM's investigative reports—results from background investigations—but as of August 2013 OPM had not yet implemented metrics to measure the completeness of these reports. OPM supplies about 90 percent of all federal clearance investigations, including those for DOD. For example, in May 2009 we reported that, with respect to DOD initial top secret clearances adjudicated in July 2008, documentation was incomplete for most OPM investigative reports. We independently estimated that 87 percent of about 3,500 investigative reports that DOD adjudicators used to make clearance decisions were missing at least one type of documentation required by federal investigative standards. The type of documentation most often missing from investigative reports was verification of all of the applicant's employment, followed by information from the required number of social references for the applicant and complete security forms. We also estimated that 12 percent of the 3,500 investigative reports did not contain a required personal subject interview.

At the time of our 2009 review, OPM did not measure the completeness of its investigative reports, which limited the agency's ability to explain the extent or the reasons why some reports were incomplete. As a result of the incompleteness of OPM's investigative reports on DOD personnel, we recommended in May 2009 that OPM measure the frequency with which its investigative reports meet federal investigative standards, so that the executive branch can identify the factors leading to incomplete reports and take corrective actions.[17]

In a subsequent February 2011 report, we noted that OMB, ODNI, DOD, and OPM leaders had provided congressional members with metrics to assess the quality of the security clearance process, including investigative reports and other aspects of the process.[18] For example, the Rapid Assessment of Incomplete Security Evaluations was one tool the executive branch agencies planned to use for measuring quality, or

---

[17]GAO, *DOD Personnel Clearances: Comprehensive Timeliness Reporting, Complete Clearance Documentation, and Quality Measures Are Needed to Further Improve the Clearance Process*, GAO-09-400 (Washington, D.C.: May 19, 2009).

[18]GAO, *High-Risk Series: An Update*, GAO-11-278 (Washington, D.C.: Feb. 2011).

completeness, of OPM's background investigations.[19] However, according to an OPM official in June 2012, OPM chose not to use this tool. Instead, OPM opted to develop another tool. In following up on our 2009 recommendations, as of August 2013, OPM had not provided enough details on its tool for us to determine if the tool had met the intent of our 2009 recommendation, and included the attributes of successful performance measures identified in best practices, nor could we determine the extent to which the tool was being used.

OPM also assesses the quality of investigations based on voluntary reporting from customer agencies. Specifically, OPM tracks investigations that are (1) returned for rework from the requesting agency, (2) identified as deficient using a web-based customer satisfaction survey, or (3) identified as deficient through adjudicator calls to OPM's quality hotline. However, in our past work, we have noted that the number of investigations returned for rework is not by itself a valid indicator of the quality of investigative work because DOD adjudication officials told us that they have been reluctant to return incomplete investigations in anticipation of delays that would impact timeliness. Further, relying on agencies to voluntarily provide information on investigation quality may not reflect the quality of OPM's total investigation workload. We are beginning work to further review OPM's actions to improve the quality of investigations.

We have also reported that deficiencies in investigative reports affect the quality of the adjudicative process. Specifically, in November 2010, we reported that agency officials who utilize OPM as their investigative service provider cited challenges related to deficient investigative reports as a factor that slows agencies' abilities to make adjudicative decisions. The quality and completeness of investigative reports directly affects adjudicator workloads, including whether additional steps are required before adjudications can be made, as well as agency costs. For example, some agency officials noted that OPM investigative reports do not include complete copies of associated police reports and criminal record checks. Several agency officials stated that in order to avoid further costs or delays that would result from working with OPM, they often choose to

---

[19]The Rapid Assessment of Incomplete Security Evaluations tool was developed by DOD to track the quality of investigations conducted by OPM for DOD personnel security clearance investigations, measured as a percent of investigations completed that contained deficiencies.

perform additional steps internally to obtain missing information. According to ODNI and OPM officials, OPM investigators provide a summary of police and criminal reports and assert that there is no policy requiring inclusion of copies of the original records. However, ODNI officials also stated that adjudicators may want or need entire records as critical elements may be left out. For example, according to Defense Office of Hearings and Appeals officials, in one case, an investigator's summary of a police report incorrectly identified the subject as a thief when the subject was actually the victim.

DOD Has Taken Steps to Implement Measures to Determine Completeness of Adjudicative Files

DOD has taken some intermittent steps to implement measures to determine the completeness of adjudicative files to address issues identified in our 2009 report regarding the quality of DOD adjudications. In 2009, we found that some clearances were granted by DOD adjudicators even though some required data were missing from the OPM investigative reports used to make such determinations. For example, we estimated in our 2009 review that 22 percent of the adjudicative files for about 3,500 initial top secret clearances that were adjudicated favorably did not contain all the required documentation, even though DOD regulations require that adjudicators maintain a record of each favorable and unfavorable adjudication decision and document the rationale for granting clearance eligibility to applicants with security concerns revealed during the investigation.[20] Documentation most frequently missing from adjudicative files was the rationale for granting security clearances to applicants with security concerns related to foreign influence, financial considerations, and criminal conduct. At the time of our 2009 review, DOD did not measure the completeness of its adjudicative files, which limited the agency's ability to explain the extent or the reasons why some files are incomplete.

In 2009, we made two recommendations to improve the quality of adjudicative files. First, we recommended that DOD measure the frequency with which adjudicative files meet requirements, so that the executive branch can identify the factors leading to incomplete files and include the results of such measurement in annual reports to Congress

---

[20]DOD Regulation 5200.2-R, *DOD Personnel Security Program* (Jan. 1987, incorporating changes Feb. 23, 1996).

on clearances.[21] In November 2009, DOD subsequently issued a memorandum that established a tool to measure the frequency with which adjudicative files meet the requirements of DOD regulation. Specifically, the DOD memorandum stated that it would use a tool called the Review of Adjudication Documentation Accuracy and Rationales, or RADAR, to gather specific information about adjudication processes at the adjudication facilities and assess the quality of adjudicative documentation. In following up on our 2009 recommendations, as of 2012, a DOD official stated that RADAR had been used in fiscal year 2010 to evaluate some adjudications, but was not used in fiscal year 2011 due to funding shortfalls. DOD restarted the use of RADAR in fiscal year 2012.

Second, we recommended that DOD issue guidance to clarify when adjudicators may use incomplete investigative reports as the basis for granting clearances. In response to our recommendation, DOD's November 2009 guidance that established RADAR also outlines the minimum documentation requirements adjudicators must adhere to when documenting personnel security clearance determinations for cases with potentially damaging information. In addition, DOD issued guidance in March 2010 that clarifies when adjudicators may use incomplete investigative reports as the basis for granting clearances. This guidance provides standards that can be used for the sufficient explanation of incomplete investigative reports.

Metrics Not Yet Implemented to Measure Clearance Reciprocity

While some efforts have been made to develop quality metrics, agencies have not yet implemented metrics for tracking the reciprocity of personnel security clearances, which is an agency's acceptance of a background investigation or clearance determination completed by any authorized investigative or adjudicative executive branch agency. Although executive branch agency officials have stated that reciprocity is regularly granted, as it is an opportunity to save time as well as reduce costs and investigative workloads, we reported in 2010 that agencies do not consistently and comprehensively track the extent to which reciprocity is

---

[21]GAO, *DOD Personnel Clearances: Comprehensive Timeliness Reporting, Complete Clearance Documentation, and Quality Measures Are Needed to Further Improve the Clearance Process*, GAO-09-400 (Washington, D.C.: May 19, 2009).

granted government-wide.[22] ODNI guidance requires, except in limited circumstances, that all Intelligence Community elements "accept all in-scope[23] security clearance or access determinations." Additionally, Office of Management and Budget guidance[24] requires agencies to honor a clearance when (1) the prior clearance was not granted on an interim or temporary basis; (2) the prior clearance investigation is current and in-scope; (3) there is no new adverse information already in the possession of the gaining agency; and (4) there are no conditions, deviations, waivers, or unsatisfied additional requirements (such as polygraphs) if the individual is being considered for access to highly sensitive programs.

While the Performance Accountability Council has identified reciprocity as a government-wide strategic goal, we have found that agencies do not consistently and comprehensively track when reciprocity is granted, and lack a standard metric for tracking reciprocity.[25] Further, while OPM and the Performance Accountability Council have developed quality metrics for reciprocity, the metrics do not measure the extent to which reciprocity is being granted. For example, OPM created a metric in early 2009 to track reciprocity, but this metric only measures the number of investigations requested from OPM that are rejected based on the existence of a previous investigation and does not track the number of cases in which an existing security clearance was or was not successfully honored by the agency. Without comprehensive, standardized metrics to

---

[22]In addition to establishing objectives for timeliness, the Intelligence Reform and Terrorism Prevention Act of 2004 established requirements for reciprocity, which is an agency's acceptance of a background investigation or clearance determination completed by any authorized investigative or adjudicative executive branch agency, subject to certain exceptions such as completing additional requirements like polygraph testing. Further, in October 2008, ODNI issued guidance on the reciprocity of personnel security clearances. ODNI, Intelligence Community Policy Guidance 704.4, *Reciprocity of Personnel Security Clearance and Access Determinations* (Oct. 2, 2008).

[23]Although there are broad federal investigative guidelines, the details and depth of an investigation varies by agency depending upon its mission.

[24]Office of Management and Budget, *Memorandum for Deputies of Executive Departments and Agencies: Reciprocal Recognition of Existing Personnel Security Clearances* (Dec. 12, 2005); Office of Management and Budget, *Memorandum for Deputies of Executive Departments and Agencies: Reciprocal Recognition of Existing Personnel Security Clearances* (July 17, 2006).

[25]GAO, *Personnel Security Clearances: Progress Has Been Made to Improve Timeliness but Continued Oversight Is Needed to Sustain Momentum*, GAO-11-65 (Washington, D.C.: Nov. 19, 2010).

track reciprocity and consistent documentation of the findings, decision makers will not have a complete picture of the extent to which reciprocity is granted or the challenges that agencies face when attempting to honor previously granted security clearances.

In 2010, we reported that executive branch officials routinely honor other agencies' security clearances, and personnel security clearance information is shared between OPM, DOD, and, to some extent, Intelligence Community databases.[26] However, we found that some agencies find it necessary to take additional steps to address limitations with available information on prior investigations, such as insufficient information in the databases or variances in the scope of investigations, before granting reciprocity. For instance, OPM has taken steps to ensure certain clearance data necessary for reciprocity are available to adjudicators, such as holding interagency meetings to determine new data fields to include in shared data. However, we also found that the shared information available to adjudicators contains summary-level detail that may not be complete. As a result, agencies may take steps to obtain additional information, which creates challenges to immediately granting reciprocity.

Further, in 2010 we reported that because there is no government-wide standardized training and certification process for investigators and adjudicators, according to agency officials, a subject's prior clearance investigation and adjudication may not meet the standards of the inquiring agency. Although OPM has developed some training, security clearance investigators and adjudicators are not required to complete a certain type or number of classes. As a result, the extent to which investigators and adjudicators receive training varies by agency. Consequently, as we have previously reported, agencies are reluctant to be accountable for investigations and/or adjudications conducted by other agencies or organizations.[27] To achieve fuller reciprocity, clearance-granting agencies seek to have confidence in the quality of prior investigations and adjudications.

---

[26]GAO-11-65.

[27]GAO, *Personnel Clearances: Key Factors to Consider in Efforts to Reform Security Clearance Processes*, GAO-08-352T (Washington, D.C.: Feb. 27, 2008).

Consequently, we recommended in 2010 that the Deputy Director of Management, Office of Management and Budget, in the capacity as Chair of the Performance Accountability Council, should develop comprehensive metrics to track reciprocity and then report the findings from the expanded tracking to Congress. Although OMB agreed with our recommendation, a 2011 ODNI report found that Intelligence Community agencies experienced difficulty reporting on reciprocity. The agencies are required to report on a quarterly basis the number of security clearance determinations granted based on a prior existing clearance as well as the number not granted when a clearance existed. The numbers of reciprocal determinations made and denied are categorized by the individual's originating and receiving organizational type: (1) government to government, (2) government to contractor, (3) contractor to government, and (4) contractor to contractor. The report stated that data fields necessary to collect the information described above do not currently reside in any of the datasets available and the process was completed in an agency specific, semi-manual method. Further, the Deputy Assistant Director for Special Security of the Office of the Director of National Intelligence noted in testimony in June 2012 that measuring reciprocity is difficult, and despite an abundance of anecdotes, real data is hard to come by. To address this problem, ODNI is developing a web-based form for individuals to submit their experience with reciprocity issues to the ODNI. According to ODNI, this will allow them to collect empirical data, perform systemic trend analysis, and assist agencies with achieving workable solutions.

Sustained Leadership Needed to Fully Develop and Implement Metrics to Monitor and Track Quality

As previously discussed, DOD accounts for the majority of security clearances within the federal government. We initially placed DOD's personnel security clearance program on our high-risk list[28] in 2005 because of delays in completing clearances.[29] It remained on our list until 2011 because of ongoing concerns about delays in processing clearances and problems with the quality of investigations and adjudications. In February 2011, we removed DOD's personnel security

---

[28]Every two years at the start of a new Congress, GAO issues a report that identifies government operations that are high risk due to their vulnerabilities to fraud, waste, abuse, and mismanagement, or are most in need of transformation to address economy, efficiency, or effectiveness.

[29]GAO, *High-Risk Series: An Update*, GAO-05-207 (Washington, D.C.: Jan. 1, 2005).

clearance program from our high-risk list largely because of the department's demonstrated progress in expediting the amount of time processing clearances.[30] We also noted DOD's efforts to develop and implement tools to evaluate the quality of investigations and adjudications.

Even with the significant progress leading to removal of DOD's program from our high-risk list, we noted in June 2012 that sustained leadership would be necessary to continue to implement, monitor, and update outcome-focused performance measures. The initial development of some tools and metrics to monitor and track quality not only for DOD but government-wide were positive steps; however, full implementation of these tools and measures government-wide have not yet been realized. While progress in DOD's personnel security clearance program resulted in the removal of this area from our high-risk list, significant government-wide challenges remain in ensuring that personnel security clearance investigations and adjudications are high-quality.

In conclusion, oversight of the reform efforts to measure and improve the quality of the security clearance process—including background investigations—are imperative next steps. Failing to do so increases the risk of damaging, unauthorized disclosures of classified information. The progress that was made with respect to expediting the amount of time processing clearances would not have been possible without committed and sustained congressional oversight and the leadership of the Performance Accountability Council. Further actions are needed now to fully develop and implement metrics to oversee quality at every step in the process. Chairman Carper, Ranking Member Coburn, this concludes my prepared statement. I would be pleased to answer any questions that you or other Members of the Committee may have at this time.

GAO Contacts and Acknowledgment

For further information on this testimony, please contact Brenda S. Farrell, Director, Defense Capabilities and Management, who may be reached at (202) 512-3604 or farrellb@gao.gov. Contact points for our Offices of Congressional Relations and Public Affairs may be found on the last page of this statement. GAO staff who made key contributions to

---

[30]GAO, *High-Risk Series: An Update*, GAO-11-278 (Washington, D.C.: Feb. 2011).

this testimony include Lori Atkinson (Assistant Director), Darreisha Bates, Renee Brown, John Van Schaik, and Michael Willems.

Related GAO Products

Personnel Security Clearances: Further Actions Needed to Improve the Process and Realize Efficiencies. GAO-13-728T. Washington, D.C.: June 20, 2013.

Managing for Results: Agencies Should More Fully Develop Priority Goals under the GPRA Modernization Act. GAO-13-174. Washington, D.C.: April 19, 2013.

Security Clearances: Agencies Need Clearly Defined Policy for Determining Civilian Position Requirements. GAO-12-800. Washington, D.C.: July 12, 2012.

Personnel Security Clearances: Continuing Leadership and Attention Can Enhance Momentum Gained from Reform Effort. GAO-12-815T. Washington, D.C.: June 21, 2012.

2012 Annual Report: Opportunities to Reduce Duplication, Overlap and Fragmentation, Achieve Savings, and Enhance Revenue. GAO-12-342SP. Washington, D.C.: February 28, 2012.

Background Investigations: Office of Personnel Management Needs to Improve Transparency of Its Pricing and Seek Cost Savings. GAO-12-197. Washington, D.C.: February 28, 2012.

GAO's 2011 High-Risk Series: An Update. GAO-11-394T. Washington, D.C.: February 17, 2011.

High-Risk Series: An Update. GAO-11-278. Washington, D.C.: February 16, 2011.

Personnel Security Clearances: Overall Progress Has Been Made to Reform the Governmentwide Security Clearance Process. GAO-11-232T. Washington, D.C.: December 1, 2010.

Personnel Security Clearances: Progress Has Been Made to Improve Timeliness but Continued Oversight Is Needed to Sustain Momentum. GAO-11-65. Washington, D.C.: November 19, 2010.

DOD Personnel Clearances: Preliminary Observations on DOD's Progress on Addressing Timeliness and Quality Issues. GAO-11-185T. Washington, D.C.: November 16, 2010.

Personnel Security Clearances: An Outcome-Focused Strategy and Comprehensive Reporting of Timeliness and Quality Would Provide Greater Visibility over the Clearance Process. GAO-10-117T. Washington, D.C.: October 1, 2009.

Personnel Security Clearances: Progress Has Been Made to Reduce Delays but Further Actions Are Needed to Enhance Quality and Sustain Reform Efforts. GAO-09-684T. Washington, D.C.: September 15, 2009.

Personnel Security Clearances: An Outcome-Focused Strategy Is Needed to Guide Implementation of the Reformed Clearance Process. GAO-09-488. Washington, D.C.: May 19, 2009.

DOD Personnel Clearances: Comprehensive Timeliness Reporting, Complete Clearance Documentation, and Quality Measures Are Needed to Further Improve the Clearance Process. GAO-09-400. Washington, D.C.: May 19, 2009.

High-Risk Series: An Update. GAO-09-271. Washington, D.C.: January 2009.

Personnel Security Clearances: Preliminary Observations on Joint Reform Efforts to Improve the Governmentwide Clearance Eligibility Process. GAO-08-1050T. Washington, D.C.: July 30, 2008.

Personnel Clearances: Key Factors for Reforming the Security Clearance Process. GAO-08-776T. Washington, D.C.: May 22, 2008.

Employee Security: Implementation of Identification Cards and DOD's Personnel Security Clearance Program Need Improvement. GAO-08-551T. Washington, D.C.: April 9, 2008.

Personnel Clearances: Key Factors to Consider in Efforts to Reform Security Clearance Processes. GAO-08-352T. Washington, D.C.: February 27, 2008.

DOD Personnel Clearances: DOD Faces Multiple Challenges in Its Efforts to Improve Clearance Processes for Industry Personnel. GAO-08-470T. Washington, D.C.: February 13, 2008.

DOD Personnel Clearances: Improved Annual Reporting Would Enable More Informed Congressional Oversight. GAO-08-350. Washington, D.C.: February 13, 2008.

DOD Personnel Clearances: Delays and Inadequate Documentation Found for Industry Personnel. GAO-07-842T. Washington, D.C.: May 17, 2007.

High-Risk Series: An Update. GAO-07-310. Washington, D.C.: January 2007.

DOD Personnel Clearances: Additional OMB Actions Are Needed to Improve the Security Clearance Process. GAO-06-1070. Washington, D.C.: September 28, 2006.

DOD Personnel Clearances: New Concerns Slow Processing of Clearances for Industry Personnel. GAO-06-748T. Washington, D.C.: May 17, 2006.

DOD Personnel Clearances: Funding Challenges and Other Impediments Slow Clearances for Industry Personnel. GAO-06-747T. Washington, D.C.: May 17, 2006.

DOD Personnel Clearances: Government Plan Addresses Some Long-standing Problems with DOD's Program, But Concerns Remain. GAO-06-233T. Washington, D.C.: November 9, 2005.

DOD Personnel Clearances: Some Progress Has Been Made but Hurdles Remain to Overcome the Challenges That Led to GAO's High-Risk Designation. GAO-05-842T. Washington, D.C.: June 28, 2005.

High-Risk Series: An Update. GAO-05-207. Washington, D.C.: January 2005.

DOD Personnel Clearances: Preliminary Observations Related to Backlogs and Delays in Determining Security Clearance Eligibility for Industry Personnel. GAO-04-202T. Washington, D.C.: May 6, 2004.